PowerKiDS
Readers
MY COMMUNITY
MI COMUNIDAD

A TRIP TO THE HOSPITAL

DE VISITA EN EL HOSPITAL

Josie Keogh

Traducción al español: Eduardo Alamán

PowerKiDS
press™

New York

Published in 2013 by The Rosen Publishing Group, Inc.
29 East 21st Street, New York, NY 10010

First Edition

Editor: Amelie von Zumbusch
Book Design: Ashley Drago

Traducción al español: Eduardo Alamán

Photo Credits: Cover © www.iStockphoto.com/Nicole Waring; p. 5 Sozaijiten/Datacraft/Getty Images; p. 6 Alexander Raths/Shutterstock.com; p. 9 Comstock/Thinkstock; pp. 10, 13 Monkey Business Images/Shutterstock.com; p. 14 Fotokostic/Shutterstock.com; p. 17 Minerva Studio/Shutterstock.com; p. 18 ERproductions Ltd/Blend Images/Getty Images; p. 21 © www.iStockphoto.com/Rich Legg; p. 22 Donald Joski/Shutterstock.com; p. 24 Stephen Coburn/Shutterstock.com.

Library of Congress Cataloging-in-Publication Data

Keogh, Josie.
[Trip to the hospital. English & Spanish]
A trip to the hospital = De visita en el hospital / by Josie Keogh ; [translated by Eduardo Alamán]. — 1st ed.
  p. cm. — (Powerkids readers: my community / mi comunidad)
Includes index.
ISBN 978-1-4488-7831-4 (library binding)
1. Hospitals—Juvenile literature. 2. Children—Hospital care–Juvenile literature. I. Title. II. Title: Visita en el hospital.
RA963.5.K4618 2013
362.11–dc23
                          2011052880

Websites: Due to the changing nature of Internet links, PowerKids Press has developed an online list of websites related to the subject of this book. This site is updated regularly. Please use this link to access the list: www.powerkidslinks.com/pkrc/hosp/

Manufactured in the United States of America

CPSIA Compliance Information: Batch #CS12PK: For Further Information contact Rosen Publishing, New York, New York at 1-800-237-9932

CONTENTS

CONTENIDO

Julia went to the hospital.

_____

Julia fue al hospital.

6

Her dad is sick.

_____

Su papá está enfermo.

7

Alex visits his grandpa.

_____

Alex visita a su abuelo.

Kathy sleeps there.

Kathy duerme en el hospital.

She has been there for a month.

Kathy ha estado ahí por un mes.

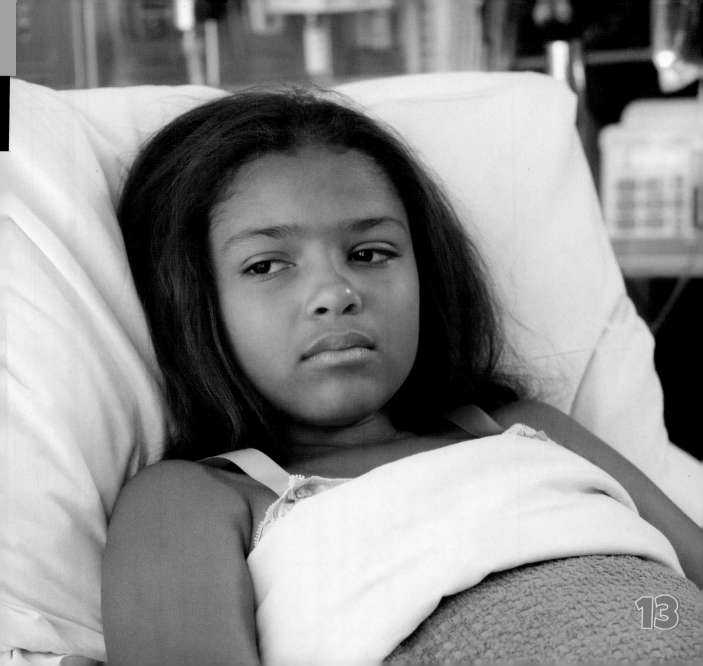

13

Ed hurt his foot.

Ed se lastima el pie.

15

Dr. Hay met with Ed.

_____

La doctora Hay atiende a Ed.

17

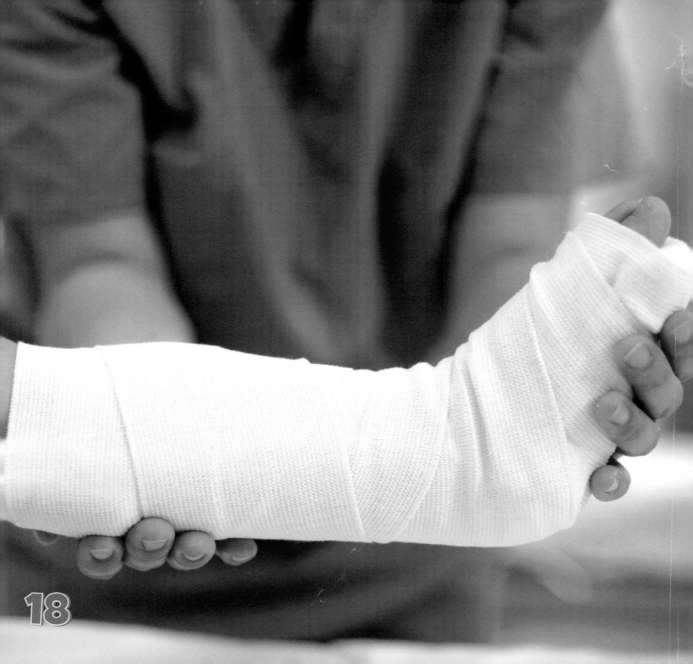

18

She gave him a cast.

_____

La doctora le pone un yeso.

Lucas met his new sister.

Lucas conoce a su
nueva hermana.

21

22

She is one day old.

La bebé tiene un día
de nacida.

WORDS TO KNOW / PALABRAS QUE DEBES SABER

doctor: A person who treats sick people.

doctor, a (el/la): una persona que trata a las personas.

nurse: A person who cares for sick people.

enfermera, o (la/el): Una persona que cuida a los enfermos.

patient: A person who is sick.

paciente (el/la): una persona que está enfrema.

INDEX

ÍNDICE